Passages
rneys through Childhood

Rights Reserved © 2008 by Lora Jo Foo

or information address:

Lora Jo Foo
Earth Passages Nature Photography
PO Box 20758
Castro Valley, CA 94546
earthpassages@yahoo.com

ISBN: 13:978-0-615-18298-8

Printed in Hong Kong. First printing May 2008

earth passages
JOURNEYS THROUGH CHILDHOOD

Lora Jo Foo

For information address:

Lora Jo Foo
Earth Passages Nature Photography
PO Box 20758
Castro Valley, CA 94546
earthpassages@yahoo.com

ISBN: 13:978-0-615-18298-8

Printed in Hong Kong. First printing May 2008

earth passages
JOURNEYS THROUGH CHILDHOOD

Lora Jo Foo

To my mother, Della

table of contents

preface

In 1991 when I first began photographing, I was fascinated with trees, particularly trees that grew through granite, those that clung onto hillsides and cliffs, and those that eked out a life in dry desert climates. "Green Tree Among Hoodoos" in Bryce Canyon, Utah (opposite page), "Heart Tree" in Bristlecone National Park, California (p.51), and the flaming tree in Abiqui Desert in New Mexico (p.24) are trees that grow and survive in harsh and barren environments. After studying and re-studying these pictures, I realized that I was photographing my early childhood.

I was born and raised in a family of eight in the inner city ghetto of San Francisco's Chinatown, the second most crowded community in the U.S. Behind the gilded golden lions and tourist-filled Grant Avenue, I lived in federal housing where I contracted tuberculosis as a child. I was raised by a mother who worked six and sometimes seven days a week, twelve hours a day in a garment sweatshop and who did not have enough time or emotional energy to give to each of her kids. Mostly abandoned by our father, my mother relied on her children to help her pay the rent and put food on the table.

Half my childhood, I was my mother's comrade-in-arms, rather than her daughter. At age 9, I worked for our uncle to help her repay her debts. At age 11, I worked with her in the sewing factory. I translated for her. I asked for directions on the buses we took. I found her the job that took her out of the Chinatown sweatshop. I was tired of taking care of her and was forever longing for someone to mother, protect and take care of me.

I wanted the Great Mother, the all-powerful, all-loving, all-nurturing, all-protecting, all encompassing earth mother. Instead, I got a mere mortal human mother. Raised in the China of the 1920's and 1930's, my mother could not break with her feudal upbringing to divorce a husband whom her daughters did not feel safe around and who siphoned off her earnings and drained her of her emotions.

To survive, I grew protective layers and a warrior's armor. I rejected all that I thought my mother embodied — her powerlessness, her dependence, her frailty. Instead I developed the swagger of a tomboy. As an adult, I became a union organizer, an attorney representing immigrant women workers, and a leader of movements. When I turned forty, however, that armor began to crack from within as the fury I held for my mother and father wanted to be released. It was at this time that I began photographing nature.

My healing from the traumas and wounds of childhood came in a number of ways. My nature photography played a major role, as did the cathartic stories I wrote about childhood, and the skilled and guiding hands of my therapists. With my photography, mother nature gives me what I did not receive from my parents – the folds of the earth that cradle, the caressing of boulders and trees, the sense of belonging, the tender and warm embrace of early morning and late afternoon sunlight, the sustenance, serenity, the safety of the womb, the attention of an only child.

My art work continues to be influenced by my childhood. I spent most of the 1990's photographing in the deserts of the Southwest. In photographing "Green Tree Among Hoodoo" in Utah, I was capturing my childhood growing up in the barrenness and harshness of an inner city ghetto. Once I understood my fascination with the desert, with its trees, its lichen clinging onto sandstone and rock, I could move onto photographing mother nature in her lush rain forests and the brilliant colors of New England autumns.

Like my writings of my journey through childhood, my nature photography tells the story of my life growing up in an inner city ghetto. These photographs are combined with my writings for the reader to understand the path I traveled to become the person I am today.

Lora Jo Foo

1

the teakettle

The teakettle shrieks, the water boiling over, hissing as it splatters the hot stove-top. Mother is holding her newly-born infant, her sixth daughter Ida, in one arm, and her other baby, her fifth daughter Daisy, in the other arm. From the strain of carrying two babies, mother's back is bent back in an arch, taut as a bow. As she puts Ida down on the brown sofa, the infant begins wailing and flailing her arms and legs. Her cries of protest pierce the air, matching those of the screeching teakettle. My mother turns toward the stove but hesitates for fear of Ida rolling off the couch. I, her almost three-year-old fourth daughter, watch wide-eyed as the teakettle screeches angrily, Ida squalls, and my mother, still holding Daisy, is caught, pulled in different directions.

2

kindergarten

On my first day of school, I cling to my mother and peer out at the other children. My sisters Betty and Dorothy are in the first and second grades. Before I began kindergarten, I'd lie on the velvet sofa with my younger sister Daisy every day, waiting for my older sisters to come home. They come home speaking a language I don't understand. They tell me that on the first day of school, some children cry and make a scene when their mothers leave them. I decide I'm not going to make a scene. I am so scared that I say nothing at all, hiding behind my mother, my fists tight around the folds of her skirt. Mother pushes me forward into a chair and silently leaves. I sit down, peering around, listening to the teacher but not understanding what she is saying. She's speaking English, the language Betty and Dorothy bring home with them. I don't understand any of the other children either. They're speaking English or Toishan, not our family dialect. I sit silent for days, maybe weeks.

3

girl-child slave

Over the years, my mother says to me, "Don't be his girl-child slave."

In the Chinese movies I saw with my mother, sometimes a mother dies and the girl-child is sold to another family as their slave. She becomes the docile servant of the young misses or the plaything of their fathers and brothers. I knew those movies were of old China, of a faraway place and a time long gone, and that girl-child slaves did not exist in America.

So I resist as best I can each time my father says to me "fetch me my slippers," "get me the newspaper," "peel me an orange," or "come here and help me pull out my white hairs." I hate that the most. Standing behind my father, smelling his greasy hair and pulling out his white strands, as if each strand pulled would slow his aging.

Sometimes, he sends me out to buy dim sum for him. I smell the delicious shrimp dumplings that he pops into his mouth while I watch and swallow only the saliva that fills mine. Sometimes he brings steaks home and fills the house with the wonderful aroma of frying meat. Dinner for us sisters comes later when our mother returns from the sewing factory to cook us rice, a dish of vegetables, dried fish so salty we could only eat a few bites, and a can of Campbell vegetable soup diluted with five cans of water to feed seven mouths.

I didn't want to become his girl-child slave. But I couldn't always stand up to my father.

bookstore uncle

One day my mother notices that my panties have a lot of discharge. Suspicious, she asks, "Does Bookstore Uncle ever touch you or play with you?" She asks reluctantly, as if she does not want to hear the answer.

Bookstore Uncle owned the Culture Bookstore on Jackson Street, one block from our apartment in the Ping Yuen complex. I was nine when my mother sent me to him as repayment for her debts. He wasn't really a blood relative. He was from the same village in China as my mother, so he was part of our extended family. Because he was family, my mother borrowed money from him often when she could not make ends meet. I ended up working for him for two years until my mother needed me at the sewing factory.

Working on weekends and after school, my job was to straighten out the magazine racks, stock the shelves, sweep the floors, dust. Bookstore Uncle carried comics of every kind and I would read them all day long. He also sold row upon row of Playboy and other girlie magazines that young Chinese men came to flip through and buy. When I straightened these out on the shelves, I never looked at what was inside.

When the store closed at 9 or 10 p.m., I would run as fast I as could the two blocks back to the Ping Yuen. One night I saw the Dirty Old Man of Chinatown standing outside looking at me through the window. I hid as best I could behind the racks, peeking out every few minutes to see if he'd gone. But he waited for me. The Dirty Old Man had a potbelly that protruded out of the red t-shirt that he always wore under his open tweed overcoat. He was unkempt, unshaven, and overweight, with thick, fat lips. He followed little girls who walked alone down Chinatown streets. He had followed my sister Dorothy and he had followed me. After what seemed like forever, I peeked out around the counter one more time and saw he was gone. I ran home as fast as I could.

Bookstore Uncle was a horny old man. On the street when he saw a well-endowed woman, he panted after her, his brow breaking out in sweat as he walked a little faster to keep pace with her. He wasn't interested in a little girl. So I could answer my mother, "No, he's never played with me." Would my mother have pulled me out of the bookstore had I answered, "Yes?" I was part of the repayment plan for the family debt.

5

white bread

One morning, as mother is packing our lunches, I yell from the bedroom, "Mom, don't make me a sandwich, I want to come home for lunch." Commodore Stockton Elementary School is two-and-a-half blocks away, close enough for me to walk home for lunch. I just want my mother to myself for once. I look forward to going home. Because I come home, my mother returns from the sewing factory also. The house is empty and quiet. It's just the two of us. I sit at the kitchen table waiting for her to serve me lunch. She puts a piece of white bread, Wonderbread or Kilpatrick's, spread with mayonnaise on a plate and hands it to me with a glass of water. My face falls. I am almost in tears.

"That's all, mom? That's it?" I say, my voice cracking and full of disappointment.

"I used up all the lunch meat this morning making your sisters' sandwiches," she says.

I never come home again for lunch.

23

6

the bank account

My father is waiting for me. I'd just come home from school and no one else is home. "We're going to the bank," he says, "get your savings book, I need the money." Over the years, my father would give me his change, a nickel here, a dime and quarter there, and I carefully would put them into a bank account. I think, *this is my money. He gave it to me.* But I'm not sure. *Maybe it isn't my money. After all, he had earned it somewhere.* I'm scared and don't want to go anywhere with him.

"Go on, get your account book," my father barks at me as he disappears down the hallway into his bedroom.

Desperate and terrified, I move slowly towards the front door. I reach for the chain and silently, very slowly, slide it out of its slot and lower it, one link at a time. The metallic sound of the chain echoes loudly in my ears, competing with the sound of my pounding heart. I lower each link until the chain dangles free. My hands still trembling, I reach for the door handle and that is when I hear his muffled laugher behind me. He is so close that I feel his breath on the back of my neck and smell the grease he uses on his hair. "Trying to sneak out, are you?" his laugh is saying to me. Maybe he grabs my hands or pushes against the door. I don't remember. The rest is like a dream.

"Come on," he says, and in silence we walk down Grant Avenue to the Bank of America on Sacramento Street. My father cleans out my bank account, all $35 worth. *Has the teller seen this before*, I wonder, *a father robbing his daughter?* In silence, we walk back down Grant and up Pacific Avenue to our apartment.

six churches for six sisters

My parents were not Buddhists or Taoist. They hung a picture of the Kitchen God up for good luck and each Spring swept the graves of the ancestors. But I needed to believe that there was an almighty God, something bigger than all of us to explain why we existed.

In junior high school, each of us sisters chose our own God. I became an Episcopalian. Betty and Dorothy became Presbyterians. Ann was a Methodist. Ida became an Evangelist. We went in different directions, choosing our churches based on the friends we had.

I tried being a devout Christian. A few times I prayed before going to bed. I would kneel before my bed with my hands together. But when my mother saw me kneeling to God she chuckled, wondering what someone as young as I knew about these things. Unsettled by her reaction, I stopped praying at home but continued going to church.

My church was the True Sunshine Episcopal Mission, two blocks from our Ping Yuen housing complex. I attended Sunday mass and also the Saturday morning recitations in the small chapel. One Saturday, I was the only person who came for the recitations. I wanted to leave but felt pinned to my seat. Father Chesterman was already sitting up on the dais. I stared at the door, hoping someone would walk in. But no one did. Father Chesterman began the service anyway. He read a verse and I, with my parched, dry mouth, managed to squeak out a refrain. This went on for an hour, an eternity, with his reading a verse and waiting for my squeak of a response. When the service ended I bolted for the door, never to return again to Saturday recitation.

For all the years that I was part of his church, Father Chesterman never asked me about my parents, what they did, where we lived, how we lived, or how I was doing in school. He might have cared about my soul but not, it seemed, much else.

8

a chinese who can't speak chinese!

Chinatown in the 1950's and 60's was populated mainly with Chinese from the Fourth District of Kwangtung Province who spoke the Toishan dialect. My family were Lung Do from the Sun Yat Sen District and spoke the Lung Do dialect. I never understood the Fourth District dialect. When my mother sent us out to buy meat or vegetables, she wrote in Chinese characters on a small piece of paper what she wanted. I handed the piece of paper to the butcher who handed me back the meat with change. Sometimes my mother would bring me back to the butcher and shout at him because he gave me less change than he should have.

The clerks would mutter, "Humph! A Chinese who can't speak Chinese!" Every time I went back to their stores with my mother I would make sure to speak Lung Do very loudly to her so they would know that I did speak Chinese. Only the fishmongers treated us well. In one store, most of them spoke Lung Do. My mother pointed out the ones who were doctors in China but, because they didn't speak English, in the U.S. they chopped off heads and skinned and filleted fish.

9

the pings

Before we moved into the Pings, we were evicted from one basement apartment after another when my father couldn't pay the rent. Sometime in 1953, when the Ping Yuen housing projects were built along Pacific Avenue, our family of six – mother, father, and four daughters – moved in. This was our home for the next sixteen years.

The Pings, as the kids outside Chinatown called the projects, were seven story concrete and cement structures. The outside corridors, the stairwells, and the apartment walls were concrete, cold to the touch. The living room, kitchen, bedrooms, and bathroom of our three bedroom apartment were covered with dark brown linoleum tiles that didn't warm up no matter how long we stood on them. Only in the summers did things change, when the sunshine came streaming through the latticework of the windowpanes, hitting the floor in well-defined squares and warming the cold tiles. We sisters each had our own square to sit in.

10

under the covers

In grammar school I loved reading books, especially Westerns and stories about crossing the plains in a covered wagon, sleeping under a wide, star-filled sky, a young girl falling in love with the scout. I daydreamed about living in a small Western town with wooden planks and riding horses. At night when all the lights in the apartment were out, I'd lie under my blanket and read with a flashlight.

One night, my dad surprises me. I hear him coming down the hall and I quickly turn off my flashlight, pulling the blanket over my head and shutting my eyes. I hear him enter my bedroom and I lie motionless. I feel the blanket slowly being lifted off me. He leans down to look into my face. He is so close I can hear his breathing and smell the oil he uses on his hair. He watches me pretending to be asleep. He watches for a long, long time. Finally I feel the blanket being lowered over me again and hear him softly laughing as he turns to leave. It isn't a fatherly laugh.

In my teens, I woke one night to find my dad doing something with my bed-spread. I thought he was pulling the covers over me but realized that his hands were pulling the covers where my crotch was. I turned over, pretending he was trying to pull the covers over me and he pretended it also and went away.

the basement of cameron house

At the turn of the 20th century, girls were stolen from their homes in China, brought to the brothels of San Francisco's Chinatown, and forced into prostitution. Donaldina Cameron, a white woman missionary, raided the brothels to rescue the slave girls, taking them into tunnels underneath Chinatown that led into the basement of Cameron House, a three story red brick building on Sacramento and Powell Streets. Cameron House became the home for these girls. As a teenager, I learned about Cameron House from my sisters Betty and Dorothy. By then, there were no more brothels and girl-child prostitutes. But in my psyche the basement of Cameron House remained a refuge, a safe haven for girl-child slaves.

12

inverness woods

I sit gulping in the fresh air, my head between my knees. I wait for the dizziness and chills to pass and the breeze to dry the sweat from my body. By then, mass will be over and the congregation spilling out of the church.

It happens every Sunday like this. The mass with its breaking of bread and drinking of wine drones on. I feel faint from the heat in the church and from kneeling and standing, kneeling and standing. A chill comes over me even though I am sweating under my choir robe. The sounds of church music and the minister's sermon seem to come from a long distance away. The sunlit church turns dim. I kneel for as long as I can and at the last moment stand up and walk down the aisle, my eyes trying to focus because the church has gone dark on me. I make it outside, feeling relieved that I have not embarrassed myself by dropping in a dead faint in front of the congregation.

This particular Sunday, the True Sunshine Episcopal Mission of Chinatown is in Inverness, California, joining its sister church in worship. This time, just like the others, I stand up and walk down the aisle before I faint. I find a shady spot to sit and gulp in the air of the surrounding woods. As I recover, I become aware of the smell of the earth and the sound of bird song. In front of me the woods slowly come into focus. Beckoning woods. They are not like Golden Gate Park where if one walks only a little ways, one comes upon the cement and sidewalks of the Richmond or Sunset Districts of the city. These woods stretch out endlessly.

As I look, I see a trail leading into the woods. As my little sister Ida and my best friend Doris come out of the church with other little girls of my age, I gather them together. The adults of both congregations are busy visiting with each other. No one pays attention to the group of six little Chinese girls whom I am leading single file into the woods.

We are in our Sunday best. As we walk in our patent leather shoes, weed seeds burl into our white stockings. We pick them off with our tender fingers. We do not complain because that is part of the adventure. We walk over soft earth covered with fallen pine needles, and are enveloped in their pungent smell. All about us are tall brown trees, black earth and pinecones. After some time has passed, we come upon a large house in the woods and pause a while looking at it. The front door opens. A slender man in his forties, wearing blue jeans and a t-shirt, smiles at us and invites us in for coffee. He is tickled. What a sight. Six little Chinese girls marching single file through the woods.

Doris tugs at my sleeve. "Don't go in," she says. I ignore her. Doris pays too much attention to all the scary stories her mother reads her from the Chinatown newspapers about little girls disappearing into the night. The line of little girls follows me into the house. It is a pink house. Everything in it is pink — the sofa, the wallpaper, the kitchen table where we sit drinking coffee. *Just like adults*, I think, *and having such a nice conversation with this nice man*. I comment about the pink and the man tells us that he even has a pink bathtub. Would we like to see? And again, this time using the village dialect, Doris says "don't follow him into the bathroom." I would have none of it. Off we troop into the bathroom and marvel at the small pink bathtub and pink toilet with the fluffy pink toilet plastic seat cover. We take turns sitting on the soft toilet seat.

When it is time to leave, we thank the man for his hospitality. He sees us to the door and in single file the little girls follow me on down the trail. Eventually, we come out of the woods and onto a beach where we discover our two congregations picnicking. We have been gone for hours. Seeing us, Father Chesterman storms over, anger on his face. "Where have you been?" he demands. I am so nervous a giggle escapes my lips.

13

marry a dog, follow the dog

"Mom," I plead, "you have to divorce him. Why can't you just divorce him?"

My father didn't help pay the bills. Instead, he gambled away my mother's hard earned wages. Because of his gambling, my mother had to leave her eldest daughter Gina behind in China. My dad immigrated in 1938. After he served in the U.S. Army during World War II, the government allowed him to bring my mom and Gina over to join him. In 1948, Mom and Gina traveled from their village to Hong Kong to meet my dad. But in Hong Kong, he had gambled away so much money that he only had passage money for my mom.

In the U.S., my mother gave birth to six more daughters. She and my father kept trying for a boy. Being around his daughters reminded my father of what he didn't have, a male heir. So he left us as often as he could and was gone for many months out of each year. He worked as a waiter in Chinese restaurants in small towns throughout California, Colorado and Alaska. He came back only when he was out of a job or money.

When my father left us, sometimes he sent money home. Mostly he didn't. When he came home, any money he made he gambled away in the casinos up in Reno or in the Chinatown gambling houses. He borrowed from our relatives, leaving my mom with the burden of repaying his debts. Once another father came looking for my dad, pounding on our door and demanding his money back. "I have children to feed too," the man yelled.

My parents fought whenever my father came home, leaving my mother in tears every time. When he couldn't get money from her, he would go on rampages, tearing up family photos and destroying things that she held dear.

But my mom stayed with him. She could not overcome tradition. Marry a chicken, follow the chicken; marry a dog, follow the dog.

14

her hair smells!

After my seventh sister Ann was born, my mother went to work full-time in the sewing factories. Once she started working, she had little time for us. Six and seven days a week, ten to twelve hours a day she was in the sewing factory. One day in grammar school, I was standing in line waiting to return to class from morning recess. A girl behind me said to her friend, "Her hair smells!" She was talking about me. My mother used to give us our baths and wash our hair. But now we never saw her. I could feel my face turning red at the girl's comment. That day I went home and learnt how to wash my own hair.

15

I want to live with you

When I worked for my uncle and aunt in their bookstore, I often ate dinners with them in their apartment. They cooked shrimp in black bean sauce, ginger and scallion steamed fish, spareribs, and things that my mother couldn't always afford to cook for us. One day my mother comes over while we are eating dinner.

"Do you want to live with your aunt and Bookstore Uncle?" my mother asks.

Living with my aunt and uncle meant I would get the attention of an only child and be well fed. As I look at my mother standing on the other side of the dining table as she waits for my answer, what lies between us is the food. I feel she is testing my loyalties to her and at the same time I feel she is pushing me out of her house.

Finally I say, "No, I want to live with you."

the sewing factory I

Before we sisters started working with my mother, I'd come to the sewing factory on a Sunday and find her alone. The only sound in the factory came from her machine. She sat hunched over it, sewing, while the other women spent their Sundays with their families.

The summer before entering junior high school, I went to work in the sewing factory with my mom. That summer I joined my sisters Betty and Dorothy, who had started working there the year before. Six days a week I sat at that sewing machine from 9 a.m. in the morning until 10 p.m. at night.

At age 11, I was so small you couldn't see me sitting behind the industrial sewing machine. When I first sat down to sew and my feet pushed the pedal, the needle raced up and down so fast and the feeder pulled my cloth in so quickly that I lost control and ended up sewing what looked like jagged peaks. Eventually, I learned how to control the speed of the machine by controlling the pressure I put on the foot pedal.

Our sewing factory was kitty corner to the Ping Yuen where we lived. It was in a building that was once a residential hotel. The walls between the rooms on the second floor had been torn down and made into two large, airy rooms with light streaming through the large windows on sunny days and florescent lights adding more brightness on cloudy days. Rows and rows of sewing machines, each operated by a Chinese woman, lined the rooms.

Once a week a white man from the designer's firm would come and inspect the garments and speak to the boss. He'd walk down the aisle of sewing machines and stop in front of mine to ask "What are you going to be when you grow up?" And I'd always pipe up with "a doctor!" When he asked my sister Dorothy, she just glared at him.

We sisters were never paid any wages. Rather, what my mother made on piece rates more than tripled because she was able to assemble three or four times as many garments in a day with us as her assembly line. With us helping out, she stopped working on Sundays.

17

the sewing factory II

The summer when I was twelve, my church sent me to summer camp at The Bishop's Ranch in Healdsburg, California. For one wonderful week I played games like other children, went hiking and swimming in the Russian River, lay on the grass staring up at the wide expanse of blue sky and white clouds that lazily drifted by, gazed at the Big Dipper and stars at night, shared a cabin with three other girls, gossiped about boys, and had no responsibilities other than being a child. In discovering the outdoors, I felt like a caged bird set free.

The week ended all too quickly and there I was back in the sewing factory. Had our factory been windowless or had bars and drapes over the doors and windows like so many others, perhaps I wouldn't have been so miserable. Instead, our factory was up on the second floor with large windows facing an expanse of tree-lined parking lot. Through the open windows I could hear birds singing and the rustling of leaves in the wind, feel the occasional breeze, and imagine the sunshine on my skin. I had been proud of working alongside my mother, helping her pay the rent, putting food on the table. Now, I felt trapped. I yearned to be out in the sunshine, among the trees, under a blue sky and in the breeze.

18

da, dis, and dat

"Th," says the teacher, standing in front of the class with her tongue between her teeth, blowing air and the "th" sound at us. In junior high I first became aware of our Chinatown accents. We didn't pronounce the "th" sound in "the," "that," "this," "these," "they," "there." Instead we said da, dat, dis, dese, dey and dere. We dropped the endings of words. We'd say to each other "Will your mudder and fadder let you go to dat schoo? My mudder dinks its bedder dan da Chinatown schoo." So every day our teacher spent half of English class having us "th" along with her and ending our words with full stops to get the "t" or "d" ending out of our mouths. She was trying to drill the Chinatown out of us.

19

home economics

Our first project was sewing an apron for ourselves. I had already worked a whole summer in the sewing factory and everyday after school headed there to sew linings into jackets, set collars and sleeves onto blouses, sew zippers into skirts and pants. The Home Economics teacher did not ask us if we knew how to sew. Instead, she spent the first day showing us how to thread a sewing machine. How could I tell her I didn't need a tracing wheel to sew a straight line or half a semester to sew an apron?

Sensing that the lives of immigrant families and their children who worked twelve-hour days behind industrial sewing machines would be foreign and thus incomprehensible to her, I said nothing. Besides, I couldn't tell an adult white woman how silly her Home Economics class was when compared to the real life experiences of her students.

your IQ isn't high enough

Marina Junior High divided us by IQ levels. The "EX" and "IX" kids with the highest IQ's came from professional white families or were third or fourth generation Chinese Americans. The "2Y" kids of average IQ, where I was tracked, were white kids from working class Italian families and second generation American-born Chinese from Chinatown. Our parents were immigrants working as dishwashers, waiters, seamstresses, grocery store clerks and janitors. Our Chinatown accents gave us away. The "3Y" and "4Z" kids with the lowest IQs were new immigrants who spoke Chinese to each other or were simply misdiagnosed.

In the eighth grade, my "2Y" friends Nancy, Sylvia, and I approached our junior high school counselor to ask permission to take certain math and science courses. We needed them to enter Lowell High, San Francisco's college prep school. I was a straight "A" student and determined to be the doctor I daydreamed of being while working in the sewing factory.

But the counselor responded, "Your IQ isn't high enough. You can't take those courses." I argue with him. "But we can pass those courses. We take classes with the "EX" and "1X" kids in La'in and they cheat off our tests. We're as smart as them." "In what?" he asks. "In La'in," comes our response.

"In what?" he asks again. "In La'in" we chorus back, this time looking at each other. I spell it out for him: "L-A-T-I-N." "Oh, Latin" he says, "well girls, like I said, your IQ isn't high enough. Sorry." I am crushed. I hate the counselor. After that, each night instead of studying, I am out on the streets.

21

dad's homecoming

I say to the driver, "795 Pacific Avenue, please," as my father and I step into the taxicab. He has a heavy suitcase with him so he decides not to take the bus home. Moments earlier, he had gotten off a Greyhound bus after days of traveling from Denver, Colorado where he worked as a waiter in a Polynesian Restaurant. The cab driver, a white man, pulls out of the Greyhound station as the sky is turning dark.

Sitting next to my father in the back seat, I think about how surprised I was when he stepped off the bus. He is much shorter than I remember him. In the two years he has been gone, I have grown.

When my father is away, I miss him. I am proud when he shows me the poems he has published, his picture printed alongside them in the Canadian Chinese magazines. He always encouraged us to draw and enter art contests. When it was apparent that Dorothy was the budding artist among us, he gave her a lot of time and attention, helping her develop her drawing skills. I am glad he has come home.

I stare out the window deep in thought, but as the cab passes rows of factory buildings and warehouses, I realize that the taxicab driver isn't heading for Chinatown. He is driving through empty streets. He slows down and peers into the dark looking for "795." I shift in my seat and my dad and I look at each other. I say again to the cab driver, "795 Pacific." The cab driver says, "Oh! I'm sorry. I thought you said Fifth Street. But don't worry, I won't charge you full fare." He heads back towards Chinatown and after he drops us off in front of the Ping Yuen, my dad and I look at each other but again we do not speak. He knew and I knew that this cab driver had tried to cheat us because we were Chinese. My father hadn't spoken when we both got into the cab. Instead, a fourteen-year-old girl had spoken for him. The taxicab driver knew my father was an immigrant.

22

the picket line

"Mom," I ask, "why don't you sue your boss?"

One day as I was riding the bus home from school, I saw a picket line of Chinese women on Stockton Street. The women were in their forties and fifties - my mother's age. They carried signs and were marching in front of the Margaret Rubel sewing shop trying to unionize their factory. I was exhilarated. Here were Asian immigrant women standing up for themselves. The next day I went into my high school cafeteria and tried to convince other students to come out and support these women. In my mind, the union became a safe haven, a haven for girl-child slaves and oppressed immigrant women.

Then I met Richard, a young law school graduate who was studying for the bar. I told him about the Chinatown sweatshops, about the 12-hour days, and child labor. I grew excited as we spoke and started planning how to get my mother and her co-workers to file suit against her sewing shop. "Whoa, let's not get carried away," said the lawyer-to-be, trying to dampen my enthusiasm. Undeterred, I tried convincing my mother to sue her boss anyway.

"What? The boss will hate me forever" responded my mom. My first attempt at labor organizing was a failure.

23

the peace rug

One year, a federally funded summer youth program comes to Chinatown to provide activities for low-income kids. My sister Daisy, one year younger than me, gives such a low estimate of our family income that she gets into the program. I am rejected. Neither of us knows what mother makes each year, but I give too high an estimate.

As part of the program, Daisy is given materials and tools for an art project. She designs a rug with a peace symbol. Every night for weeks on end Daisy stays up late into the night working on her rug. As the family sleeps, I sit next to her watching as she hooks yarn through the tiny holes of the mesh backing and one hole at a time pulls the yarn through and knots them off. We sit silently, I leaning very close and intently watching. I wait for her to tire and to offer me a chance to work on her rug. My fingers tingle, yearning to reach out to hold the hooking tool. But Daisy ignores me. Night after night she ignores me while I sit watching her work, my yearning painful and palpable, until she finally finishes her rug.

a fish out of water

In high school, I was a hippie, a fish out of water. Copying the white Flower Children, I walked through Chinatown streets barefooted. But Chinatown streets were sticky with fish scales, chicken feathers and blood swept each day from the floors of the live fish and poultry markets. Chinatown's immigrants were appalled. No one in America walked around barefoot.

I stopped walking around Chinatown barefoot.

25

defying the "man"

I'm hitchhiking with my girlfriends on Columbus Avenue, just at the point where Chinatown ends and the mostly Italian neighborhood of North Beach begins. Two policemen see us, come over, and ask me when I came to this country and where I live. They don't ask my white friends. I feel my anger rising at the assumption that I am a foreigner, a runaway. I grit my teeth and answer that I was *born* here and didn't live far.

Fuming, I walk sandwiched between the two policemen to our Ping Yuen apartment, my head barely above their waists. My sister Dorothy answers the policeman's knock. He starts to enter the apartment but I jump in front of him and rage: "Who invited you in? Do you have a search warrant?" I storm off to my bedroom, grab a stack of my reports cards, and come back to the living room, where the police have entered anyway, and wave the cards in front of their faces, shouting "I'm a straight A student. See this, A's every semester! How dare you treat me like this?"

The next time it is the California Highway Patrol who stop me. I am hitchhiking on Highway 101. The officer calls my house to ask if my parents would come get me. My father is home. He doesn't speak English, doesn't drive, doesn't know anyone who owns a car or even where Highway 101 might be. He is furious. He tells Dorothy, who answered the phone, to tell the officer to let me go. I don't go home that night, waiting out my father's storm. A month later my mother and I end up in front of a juvenile court judge, who admonishes me about hitchhiking on the freeway. My mother sits through the hearing, mortified, with no interpreter to translate for her. I sit facing the judge, spitting out a "yes" or "no" in response to his questions.

The Chinese American court clerk stares at me in disbelief. Chinese girls are raised to be filial and obedient. They don't get hauled into court, unrepentant and defiant.

26

ms. chinatown, U.S.A.

"Why don't you enter the Ms. Chinatown U.S.A. beauty pageant? I think you have a good chance of winning," says my father.

My father, who didn't give a damn about me most of my childhood, suddenly has aspirations for me when I am in high school.

"Dad," I reply, "Beauty pageants are sexist and degrade women and I have no intentions of entering one."

"Hmpf," he says.

27

graduation

In her junior year, my sister Daisy dropped out of high school. For me to escape poverty, I knew I had to graduate. I worked throughout high school to save for the day when I could move out of my mother's house. At night after finishing my homework, I would stay up, sometimes until dawn, sewing clothing to sell in the boutiques on Upper Grant Avenue to well-to-do hippies. When my sisters woke, they would see my latest creations hanging on the living room door. I once sold a shirt to a member of the Jim Morrison band. I developed my own clientele and custom designed clothing for them.

One of those clients owned Pasha Pillows, a business that made psychedelic pillows. When his businesses expanded, he hired my mother. At Pasha Pillows my mom earned above minimum wage for the first time and worked a normal eight-hour day like most Americans. When she worked overtime, she was even paid overtime compensation.

In June 1968, at age seventeen, I graduated from high school and moved out of my mother's house and Chinatown forever.

28

journey to alaska

"I work next to the Iron Chink!" I would say when people asked. My job was pulling salmon eggs out of the belly of the fish that moved past me on the assembly line. By the time the salmon reached me, they had already passed through the Iron Chink, the machine with rotating blades that made a "chink, chink, chink" sound as it chopped off their heads.

On April Fool's Day, 1970, I boarded a ferry with my friend Holly and traveled up the Inside Passage of Southeast Alaska to find work in the canneries. A few days later, we arrived in St. Petersburg, on the island of Mitok, where we were to stay until that October. That first week, we caught the last snowfall of the season.

St. Petersburg was a town of about 2,000 inhabitants -- native Tlinket, Norwegian settlers, and one Japanese-American family. My high school was larger than the whole town. Every summer, the town's population grew as loggers arrived and Filipino workers traveled from the Central Valley of California after picking the late spring and early summer harvest to work in the salmon canneries.

Salmon season started in July. We lived in a cabin on a beach, three miles from town and down the only road on the island. Until I got a bicycle and learned to ride, we walked the three miles to town to work and back. The side of the road where the land sloped upward into forest was covered with giant ferns and huge skunk plants, a single leaf as tall as my shoulder. When the forest cleared, it gave way to muskeg, flat marshy ground that surrounded the island. On the other side of the road were the slow flowing waters of the narrows of the Inside Passage, fishing boats chucking their way back and forth to and from town or out to sea.

Salmon was not plentiful in 1970, so when we weren't working, I went hiking. The entire island was covered with forest, so I would just set off down the dirt road to find a place to enter the woods. The interior of the island was not settled, since most everyone lived by the water. Hiking off-trail meant climbing, sliding or swinging on or over fallen moss-covered trees that crisscrossed the forest floor. I loved the feel of the thick carpet of moss as I scrambled over or jumped from fallen tree trunk to tree trunk. Because of the constant mist, the forest was clean and wet, emerald, and fresh smelling.

The salmon season ended in September. In October, when the weather turned cold, Holly and I left as we came, on the ferry, this time to Prince Rupert, Canada. From Prince Rupert, we hitchhiked to Vancouver, then across Canada to Montreal and Quebec and crossed the Canadian-U.S. border into Vermont. New England autumn was in its full glory and I wanted to soak it all up. I climbed the rolling hills and laid nude on a rock, soaking in the sun through a clearing and feeling the autumn breeze cool against my skin.

We thumbed our way through New York and Pennsylvania, headed west for California. In Denver, Colorado, we hopped on a Greyhound Bus back to San Francisco. When the familiar green rolling hills of Marin County and the city skyline came into view, I was excited to be back.

Soon after, I enrolled as an undergraduate at San Francisco State University. In my Chinese-American history class, I discovered that Chinese men had traveled to Alaska at the turn of the century to work in the salmon canneries. Their job was to chop off the heads of salmon until they were replaced by the Iron Chink! In an insular community such as San Francisco's Chinatown, no one ever spat out words like "Chink" or "Gook" at me. Imagine my surprise at discovering it wasn't the chink, chink, chink sound that gave the machine its name!

epilogue

My mother passed away in July 2007. At her funeral service, each of my sisters read a tribute to our mother. Listening to them, I realized how differently we each experienced her. Ida talked about our mother as a healer. She described the bitter herbs mom brewed for us to drink, the powders she blew into our throats, the pastes she made for us to swallow and how her example led Ida to a life as a nurse. My sister Dorothy, who went into the restaurant business, told us how, as a little girl, she spent hours watching mom prepare and cook our meals. She remembered waking up with mom in the early hours of Chinese New Year when everyone else was still asleep to make the New Year pastries.

Like my sisters, I wanted to remember the best of my mother, but my anger with her had prevented me from seeing the positive and powerful influence she had had on my life. Hearing my sisters' tributes, I realized that my mother also had influenced my life choices. When I think back on why I became a labor activist and attorney, I realize now that it started with her, with my experiencing as a young child her hard life and wanting to make the world a better place for girl-children and women. The first worker I tried to organize was my mom.

In the weeks following her death, we sisters gathered together to share memories and photos. I was struck by one photograph taken in 1972 at the San Francisco International Airport when my mother was about to fly to China for the first time in 24 years to reunite with her mother and her oldest daughter Gina. In the photo, she flashes a smile full of happiness and excitement — all emotions I don't remember ever seeing on her face.

We also shared some frank discussions about my mom and our own lives. From these exchanges, I finally understood why my mother could never be the mother I longed for. My sister Dorothy, who raised her daughter as a single mom, told me that she had thought that taking care of her daughter's everyday needs was enough to show her how much she loved her. But her daughter longed for the very thing that our mom seldom gave us – emotional support, encouragement, and tangible expressions of how important we were to her. Unlike me, Dorothy's young daughter was able to express her need for emotional support and taught my sister how to be a better mother. If Dorothy, raised in America, needed help learning to be a good mother, how much harder was it for my mom, who was raised in a culture which did not easily show emotions. I finally understood that my mother had raised us the only way she knew and did the best she could.

I was not ready to publish this book until my mom passed away. Over a year before her death, I had prepared the final manuscript and went through the motions of finding an agent and publisher. But in the deepest part of me I could not, while she was still alive, put out into the world stories so full of sadness about her.

In adulthood, my nature photography played a large role in healing the wounds from childhood. With my mother's passing, the benefit of my sisters' memories of her, and my acceptance and forgiveness of her limitations, I now am able to let go of my disappointment and bitterness over not having the mother I needed and to remember the best of her.

acknowledgement

I wrote my first story about my childhood one night in 1989 as I lay in a tent, writing by the beam of a flashlight, during a three-week trek in the Helambu-Langtang region of Nepal. Thereafter, I eked out a story or two once a year while away from home for stretches of time. It took over ten years to write these short stories. The stories were so long in the making because they were painful to recall.

I took the first photograph I considered art in 1991. It also took me ten years to build a body of photographic work large enough for exhibition and for this book. It was hard to find uninterrupted stretches of time to disappear into the woods and mountains to photograph because of my busy life as a civil rights attorney and labor activist. I gave birth to these photographs as I began healing through psychotherapy. Photography became a medium through which my emotions were able to surface as I slowly began opening my heart, laying bare my emotions, and removing the protective layers and armor that had encased and was suffocating me and suppressing my creativity.

My ex-husband, Andy, supported me through all these endeavors. The salary I earned as a nonprofit attorney could not have paid for all my travels, photo equipment, and the materials needed to build an inventory of framed photographs. My deepest and most heartfelt gratitude goes to him for his support, financial as well as in so many other ways. In fact, it was Andy who, during our 1991 rafting trip down the Colorado River in the Grand Canyon, put a Nikon in my hands and encouraged me to continue photographing after he saw the images I took from that trip. Andy became my greatest fan and severest critic, giving me honest and frank critiques that served to improve my art over the years.

I thank my Chabot College photography instructors, Dan Leonardi and Kate and Geir Jordal, who taught me about depth of field, shutter speeds, focal lengths, composition, lighting, and color printing. I especially thank Dan who patiently assisted me in the darkroom while I spent hours getting the color cast and density of each print just right.

I thank William Ramírez from Design Action Collective who did a fantastic job in designing this book so the magic of the stories and images come through in the way I meant them to. I thank my older sisters, Betty and Dorothy, for reading the first drafts of my stories for accuracy in dates, locations, and the like. Thanks also to all my sisters for sharing their memories of mom with me. I am very grateful to my friends Khadija Pierce, Charlotte Fishman, Patricia Lee, and Kathy Goldman for reading the finished manuscript and giving valuable advice and suggestions. Finally, I thank my editor, Jo Ellen Green Kaiser, for the wonderful job she did in helping me shape my childhood stories into powerful vignettes.

lora jo foo
Castro Valley, California
2008

list of plates

Date Due

Cornerstones of Freedom

The Story of
THE
LITTLE
BIGHORN

By R. Conrad Stein

Illustrated by David J. Catrow III

 CHILDRENS PRESS, CHICAGO

Library of Congress Cataloging in Publication Data

Stein, R. Conrad.
  The story of the Little Bighorn.

  (Cornerstones of freedom)
  Summary: Describes the bloody battle known as
"Custer's last stand," in which an army of Sioux
Indians led by Sitting Bull fought off an attack
by the United States cavalry, leaving no survivors
among the soldiers in Custer's command.
    1. Little Big Horn, Battle of the, 1876 — Juvenile
literature. [1. Little Big Horn, Battle of the, 1876.
2. Sitting Bull, Dakota chief, 1831-1890. 3. Custer,
George Armstrong, 1839-1876. 4. Dakota Indians — Wars,
1876. 5. Indians of North America — Wars] I. Catrow,
David J., ill. II. Title. III. Series.
E83.876.S73 1983   973.8'2   83-6594
ISBN 0-516-04663-2   AACR2

Never before had Plains Indians gathered in such numbers. Rows of tepees stretched along the Rosebud River. They formed a camp that measured five miles long and three miles wide. Nearly all the nations of the Sioux were there. So were the Cheyenne, the Arapaho, and the Blackfoot. In the past, some of those tribes had been enemies. But today they assembled peacefully. They had been summoned by the great Sioux chief Sitting Bull.

Sitting Bull was famous throughout the Indian world. He had once marched defiantly in front of soldiers' rifles as they blazed at an Indian war party. There he sat on the ground, filled his pipe, and lit it. Bullets whistled inches from his head. But the Sioux chief refused to budge until he had smoked a full bowl. As a high priest, Sitting Bull was known to have visions that could probe into the future. He often wandered into the hills and stayed there many days and nights. Those lonely vigils helped him to see a different world, a spirit world, where he could learn what the future held for his people.

He once claimed that when he walked barefoot on the soil, he could "hear the very heartbeat of the holy earth."

In the spring of 1876, Sitting Bull presided over the fifteen thousand men, women, and children who had gathered at the Rosebud. Four thousand warriors were ready to fight. The Sioux chief needed to call on his deepest spiritual powers. Hoping for a vision from the spirit world, he endured the agonizing ritual of the Sun Dance.

Just before daylight, Sitting Bull climbed to the top of a hill. He faced east, toward the rising sun. At his back stood a sacred pole. In a sing-song voice, he began to wail ancient prayers. While a circle of medicine men watched, another Sioux brave took out a knife. He cut a piece of skin from Sitting Bull's right wrist. Then he dug the knife into Sitting Bull's wrist once more. Again and again the knife slashed Sitting Bull's arm. Blood oozed from the wounds. The pain he felt must have been terrible. But Sitting Bull never flinched. He never even seemed to notice the steel blade gouging his skin. Instead, he continued praying in his monotonous, sing-song voice. When his right arm had been cut fifty times, Sitting Bull raised his left arm for the same punishing treatment. Ignoring pain was one of the ways used by a Sioux medicine man to reach the spirit world.

When blood was flowing freely from both arms, Sitting Bull began his dance. Facing the sun, he bobbed up and down on his toes. Shunning food and water, the Sioux chief danced all day and into the night. The hundred cuts on his arms blistered with pain, but he never ceased chanting his prayer-songs. Finally, after more than twenty-four hours of dancing, Sitting Bull collapsed. He had reached the state he hoped to achieve. The Indians called it "dying a passing death."

In his trancelike sleep, Sitting Bull had a remarkable vision. He saw hundreds of white soldiers and their horses falling upside down into the Indian camp. When he awoke, the Sioux chief told the medicine men of his vision. They spoke in hushed tones and then nodded in agreement. The dream could mean only one thing—the red man soon would win a stunning victory over the white man.

At the time Sitting Bull was suffering through the Sun Dance, another warrior was riding into Montana Territory. He, too, was a man with visions. He dreamed of becoming powerful in his government. Perhaps one day he would even become the

president of the United States. His name was George Armstrong Custer.

As a boy, Custer had longed to become a soldier. When he was eighteen, he entered the military academy at West Point. His performance as a student was dismal. Custer graduated with the worst grades of anyone in his class. At the time he graduated, the United States was locked in a bloody Civil War. Custer hurried off to the fighting front. There his fortunes skyrocketed. The young officer led his troops to glory in battles at Gettysburg, Cold Harbor, Yellow Tavern, and Five Forks. At twenty-three, he became the youngest general in the Union army. His bravery won him a chestful of medals and fame in both the North and the South.

After the Civil War, Custer stayed in the army. Like all officers who elected to remain in uniform, he accepted a peacetime demotion. He soon worked his way up to the rank of colonel, however. Transferred to the western frontier, Custer achieved even greater fame as an Indian fighter. Eastern newspapers printed stories of his glorious victories over the "savages." His popularity increased when he published an autobiography called *My Life on the Plains.* The book told of his battles with Indians.

Despite his successes, Custer made enemies in the army. Many rival officers said he was not a brilliant commander. They called him a glory-seeker and claimed that he often risked the lives of his men by rushing into battle. But in fifteen years as an officer, Custer never lost a battle. His troops always seemed to attack at the right place and at the right time.

Custer's critics said his string of victories was due to
what they called the "Custer luck." Like a winning
card player, Custer always managed to draw the
more-powerful hand. Over the years, the Custer
luck became known and talked about by every
soldier in the United States cavalry. Perhaps Custer
believed in his marvelous luck, too. And perhaps he
thought his luck would someday carry him to high
office in Washington.

But first Custer had to battle Sitting Bull and an
army of Plains Indians.

White invasion of Indian territory had started the
war on the Plains. This was a long-standing problem
on the American frontier. For decades, the Indians

had seen white men pushing onto their land. First came the white hunters who killed the buffalo. Then came the miners who fouled the streams. Finally, farmers strung barbed wire over land where Indians used to ride freely.

Wars broke out on the frontier. The white men had better weapons and usually had greater numbers. The Indians were forced to sign peace treaties with the government in Washington. The treaties confined the Indians to reservation lands. Many of the reservations were enormous, and the treaties promised the land to the Indians forever. One tribe was given their reservation for "as long as the rivers shall run and the grass shall grow." But even while the chiefs were signing that treaty, white settlers began moving onto their land.

In the 1870s, gold was discovered in the Black Hills. The Black Hills were sacred to the Indian people of the Great Plains. The Indians believed the land to be the resting place of the souls of their ancestors. A treaty signed by the government in Washington guaranteed that the Black Hills would be Indian land forever. Suddenly this holy ground swarmed with white gold-seekers. The furious Indians attacked the mining camps. The government sent troops, and a bloody war began.

Into this war on the Great Plains came the famous Indian fighter George Armstrong Custer.

Riding with Custer were several Indian scouts. His most trusted Indian advisor was an Arikara chief named Bloody Knife. Chief Bloody Knife studied the thousands of hoofprints and acres of chewed-up grass along the Rosebud riverbank. These signs meant that an immense band of Sioux had camped there recently.

Bloody Knife reported his findings to Custer. The colonel pondered what to do. He commanded about six hundred men. According to his scout, the Sioux force could number in the thousands. The Indian

trail led away from the Rosebud toward some high ground. Behind that high ground flowed a river the Indians called the Greasy Grass. The white men called it the Little Bighorn.

Custer mounted his horse, pointed toward the Little Bighorn, and gave the command "Forward, ho!"

For the next one hundred years, historians would argue about why Custer chose to attack even though he must have known he would be woefully outnumbered. Another large cavalry unit probed the hills near him. Custer's orders were to locate the Sioux camp and, together with that other unit, attack it. So why did Custer decide to attack the Sioux with only his six hundred men? Some historians believe that Custer wanted to win a smashing victory and see his name splashed in the newspaper headlines in the east. Others point out that Custer had always been a brave and aggressive leader. It was only natural for him to try to surprise his enemy by striking the first blow. Whatever his reasons, Custer's decision led to tragedy for his regiment and to a century of debate for historians.

Obediently, the men of the Seventh Cavalry followed their colonel toward the Little Bighorn Valley. Perhaps the men felt that their commander's luck would once again pull them through the coming battle. Many of those troops noticed their leader's new haircut. For year's Custer's trademark had been the long locks of yellow hair that flowed behind him as he raced his horse. The Indians called the colonel Yellow Hair. But at his wife's request, Custer got a short haircut just a few days before he entered this campaign. Later, some soldiers would think of the Bible story of Samson. Samson of old had the strength of one hundred men. But his strength was mysteriously linked to his long hair. When Samson's hair was cut short, his astonishing strength vanished. Some cavalry troops would soon wonder if Custer's remarkable good luck was not also, somehow, linked to his long yellow hair.

At the Little Bighorn Valley, Custer divided his forces. He sent three companies under Captain Benteen to scout his left flank. Three more companies under Major Marcus Reno rode through the valley from the south. Custer then rode over the highland with five companies to enter the valley from the north. By dividing his forces, Custer hoped to surround his enemy. However, he succeeded only in compounding his mistake. Attacking the Indians with such a small force was Custer's first mistake. Splitting that force into even smaller units was his second.

Because Custer split his forces, two separate battles were fought on the Little Bighorn River. One battle raged for two days, and one fourth of a cavalry unit was killed or wounded. The other battle

lasted a matter of minutes, and no cavalry soldier survived.

Major Reno's troops made the first contact with the Sioux. Rounding a bend in the river, the major discovered about thirty Indians. Most were boys who stood guard over a herd of horses. Following Custer's order, Reno's 130 men galloped over the shallow waters to attack. Suddenly the cavalry men saw a boiling cloud of dust rolling off the riverbank. Indian braves on horseback—perhaps a thousand of them—thundered toward the soldiers. At first the men tried to stand and fight. But Reno then ordered them to fall back. The soldiers wheeled about on their horses and scrambled toward a tree-covered hill. The retreat quickly became a rout.

One of the survivors of this battle was a captain named Edward S. Godfrey. In a magazine article written years later, the captain said, "Reno gave orders to those near him to mount and get to the bluff. . . . Owing to the noise of the firing, many did not know of the order until too late." The hill the men climbed was covered with boulders and ran practically straight up. But, as Godfrey wrote, "It was surprising to see what steep inclines men and horses clambered up under the excitement of danger."

Indian survivors also left descriptions of Reno's retreat. A Sioux named Henry Oscar One Bull said, "the soldiers were mixed up. Some got off their horses and began firing as we rode in. Others stayed mounted. Two soldiers couldn't hold their horses in all the excitement. The horses bolted, carrying their riders right into our warriors. Those soldiers didn't last long." A Cheyenne chief named Two Moon remembered, "The air was full of smoke and dust. I saw the soldiers drop back and fall into the riverbed like buffalo fleeing. They had no time for a crossing. The Sioux chased them up the hill."

At the top of the hill, the cavalry men crouched behind trees and fired at the Sioux. Dozens of horses were killed. Some soldiers used the bodies of their horses to shield themselves from Indian arrows and bullets. Others dug trenches in the rock-covered ground. They knew they were in for a long, desperate struggle.

From a distance, Sitting Bull watched the battle. The Sioux chief did not fight in the front ranks that day. Instead, he served as the religious leader and organizer of the Plains Indians. In camp, he chanted prayers for his warriors. One of those warriors was an Oglala Sioux chief named Crazy Horse.

Crazy Horse was a ferocious fighter and a brilliant leader of horsemen. Just eight days earlier he had led a huge war party to victory over a cavalry unit at the Rosebud River. At the northern end of the valley, Crazy Horse commanded almost two thousand braves. He and his men were eager to meet the next group of white soldiers foolish enough to enter the valley of the Little Bighorn.

The Indians who fought under Crazy Horse had a strange assortment of arms. Many fought with what was called a coup stick. It was a long pole used to strike or spear enemy horsemen. Other Indians had rifles. They were outdated single-shot weapons. Most of the Plains Indians were armed with trusted

bows and arrows. For three thousand years warriors throughout the world had fought with bows and arrows. This would be the last major battle in world history in which the winning side was armed primarily with bows and arrows.

In the highland, Custer and his 230 men saw the enormous Sioux camp. Countless tepees stood along the riverbank. Surely this was history's largest gathering of Plains Indians. Perhaps in one frightening instant Custer realized his mistake in tackling such a gigantic force. Students of history will always wonder if Custer entered this battle with his usual feeling of supreme confidence. Or did he ride into the valley with a single question burning in his mind—my God, what have I done?

At the riverbank, Custer and his men were quickly surrounded. Led by the hard-riding Crazy Horse, the massed braves poured in on the soldiers from every direction. The valley echoed with shrill Indian war whoops, the cracking of rifles, the neighing of terrified horses, and the dreadful screams of wounded and dying men.

From the camp, Sitting Bull looked on as a cloud of dust covered the battle scene. He did not need to watch this battle to know what the outcome would be. He had seen it in his vision during the Sun Dance.

No white soldier in the five companies commanded by Custer lived to tell his story of the fight. Years later, Indian braves were interviewed by writers. They gave vivid descriptions. A warrior named Low Dog remembered, "I called to my men, 'This is a good day to die: follow me.' As we rushed upon them, the white soldiers dismounted to fire, but they did a very poor job shooting. They held their horse reins in one arm while they were shooting, but their horses were so frightened that they pulled the men all around. A great many of their shots went up in the air and did us no harm. The white soldiers stood their ground bravely and none of them made an attempt to get away."

A Sioux named Dewey Beard was called away from the fighting against Major Reno and dashed four miles up the river to do battle against Custer. He said, "This new battle was a turmoil of dust and warriors and soldiers, with bullets whining and arrows hissing all around. Sometimes a bugle would sound and the shooting would get louder. Some of the soldiers were firing pistols at close range. Our knives and war clubs flashed in the sun. I could hear bullets whiz past my ear. But I kept going and shouting, 'It's a good day to die!' so that everyone who heard would know I was not afraid of being killed in battle."

It is not certain how Custer himself was finally brought down. A Sioux warrior named White Bull believed he was the slayer. Curiously, White Bull was Sitting Bull's nephew. He told of a hand-to-hand struggle with a single white soldier. "I charged in. A tall, well-built soldier with yellow hair and

mustache saw me coming and tried to bluff me, aiming his rifle at me. But when I rushed him he threw his rifle at me without shooting. I dodged it. We grabbed each other and wrestled there in dust and smoke. It was like fighting in a fog. This soldier was very strong and brave. . . . Finally I broke free. He drew his pistol. I wrenched it out of his hand and struck him with it three or four times on the head, knocked him over, shot him in the head, and then fired at his heart."

On June 25, 1876, the Custer luck vanished like a puff of gunsmoke. All 230 men in Custer's immediate command were killed. According to Indian reports, the battle was over in less than half an hour.

To the south, Major Reno had been joined on the hill by the three companies under Captain Benteen. Those men of the Seventh Cavalry fought the Indians in a battle that dragged on for two days. Fifty of their number died in the fighting. Still they were lucky. They were attacked near a hill that they could climb and defend. Custer, their suddenly luckless commander, had been caught on open ground.

Finally, Reno and Benteen were joined by a large cavalry unit that rode in from the south. The Indians were forced to retreat. That same large cavalry unit had intended to join Custer in the attack on the Indian camp. Had Custer waited, he might have averted tragedy.

The Little Bighorn battle was fought the year Americans celebrated their one hundredth birthday. The mood of the country was confident. Hopeful farmers streamed to what seemed to be endless empty land in the west. Few of those farmers cared that the "empty" land had been the Indians' home for centuries. Most American people believed the

Indians to be Godless savages who did not deserve the fine land that lay to the west.

A large part of the people's attitude toward the Indians had been molded by stories they read in newspapers and books. Those stories portrayed the Indians as being treacherous and cruel. The New York *Herald* of July 13, 1876, described the Indian braves at Little Bighorn as "those wild swarming horsemen circling along the heights like shrieking vultures waiting for the moment to sweep down and finish the bloody tale." A newspaper story dated July 12 claimed that an Indian named Rain-in-the-Face had killed Custer. "Rain-in-the-Face cut the heart from Colonel Custer's body and held a grand war dance around it."

Nearly every newspaper in the country claimed the battle had been an attack *by* the Sioux *on* the cavalry. Actually, Custer and his men were attacking the Sioux camp. In that camp were thousands of women and children. At least one newspaperman, however, pleaded for fairness in treatment of the Little Bighorn battle. Writing in the Boston *Transcript,* editor Wendell Phillips asked, "What kind of war is it where, if we kill the enemy it is death; if he kills us it is massacre?"

Still, most Americans chose to believe the more-sensational stories about events on the Little Bighorn. After the battle, they demanded that more soldiers be sent west to deal with the "savages."

The army quickly sent more soldiers to the frontier. They also began an investigation of the battle. The investigation revealed Custer's two major mistakes—attacking without waiting for reinforcements and dividing his forces. During the investigation, a general named Samuel Sturgis said of Custer, [He] "was a brave man, but also a very selfish man. He was insanely ambitious of glory... and had no regard for the soldiers under him."

Dozens of books and stories soon were written about the Little Bighorn battle. The battle also inspired artists to paint scenes of it. It is estimated that nine hundred different artists have painted pictures of Custer's desperate fight on the riverbank. Of course, no artist witnessed the battle. So most of the pictures are highly fictionalized. Like the books and stories, they show brave, clean-cut cavalry men fighting painted savages. The most popular painting of the battle was commissioned by the Anheuser Busch beer company. It shows Custer with a sword drawn over his head about to slay a Sioux brave. The

beer company had 150,000 lithograph copies of this painting printed. The copies were pasted on the walls of saloons and beer halls across the nation. The famous painting was called "Custer's Last Stand."

Actually, the Battle of the Little Bighorn could be considered the Plains Indians' last stand. They had won an important victory, but never again would they command such power. Shortly after the battle, the Sioux broke into smaller camps in order to hunt buffalo. The smaller lodges were easy prey for patroling cavalry troops. In the fall of 1876, soldiers under the command of General Crook raided thirty-seven Indian camps. Because of the loss of the Seventh Cavalry, the soldiers burned for revenge. Their victims included old people, children, and women.

Sitting Bull was forced to flee to Canada with a small band of followers. In his absence, other chiefs signed a peace treaty with a representative of the government in Washington. The treaty pushed the Plains Indians onto a new, smaller reservation. Worst of all, the Sioux lost the Black Hills—that sacred land that had been promised to them forever.

Gold-seekers soon flocked to the Black Hills. They were followed by ranchers, farmers, and men who hammered steel railroad tracks into wooden ties.

Now and then, these busy newcomers looked up from their work and saw bands of Indians standing motionless and gazing at the horizon. Most of them were old men and women who seemed to be lost in their dreams.

Why had those old people returned to the Black Hills? Many had come to try to hear the whispers of their ancestors, whose souls they believed rested in this eternal land. Others had come to remember the hundreds of years when Indian people rode freely over the Great Plains. And a few of the old people had come to the Black Hills to die. No government in Washington could prevent them from doing that, at least.

About the Author

R. Conrad Stein was born and grew up in Chicago. He enlisted in the Marine Corps at the age of eighteen, and served for three years. He then attended the University of Illinois, where he received a Bachelor's Degree in history. He later studied in Mexico and earned a Master of Fine Arts degree from the University of Guanajuato.

The study of history is Mr. Stein's hobby. Since he finds it to be an exciting subject, he tries to bring the excitement of history to his readers. He is the author of many other books, articles, and short stories written for young people.

Mr. Stein is married to Deborah Kent, who is also a writer of books for young readers.

About the Artist

David J. Catrow III was born in Virginia and grew up in Hudson, Ohio. He spent three years in the United States Navy as a hospital corpsman then subsequently attended Kent State University, where he majored in biology. He is a self-taught illustrator. Mr. Catrow currently lives in Hudson, Ohio with his wife Deborah Ann and daughter Hillary Elizabeth. The artist would like to thank Deborah for her constant support and inspiration.